ELEANOR *Roosevelt*

Our People

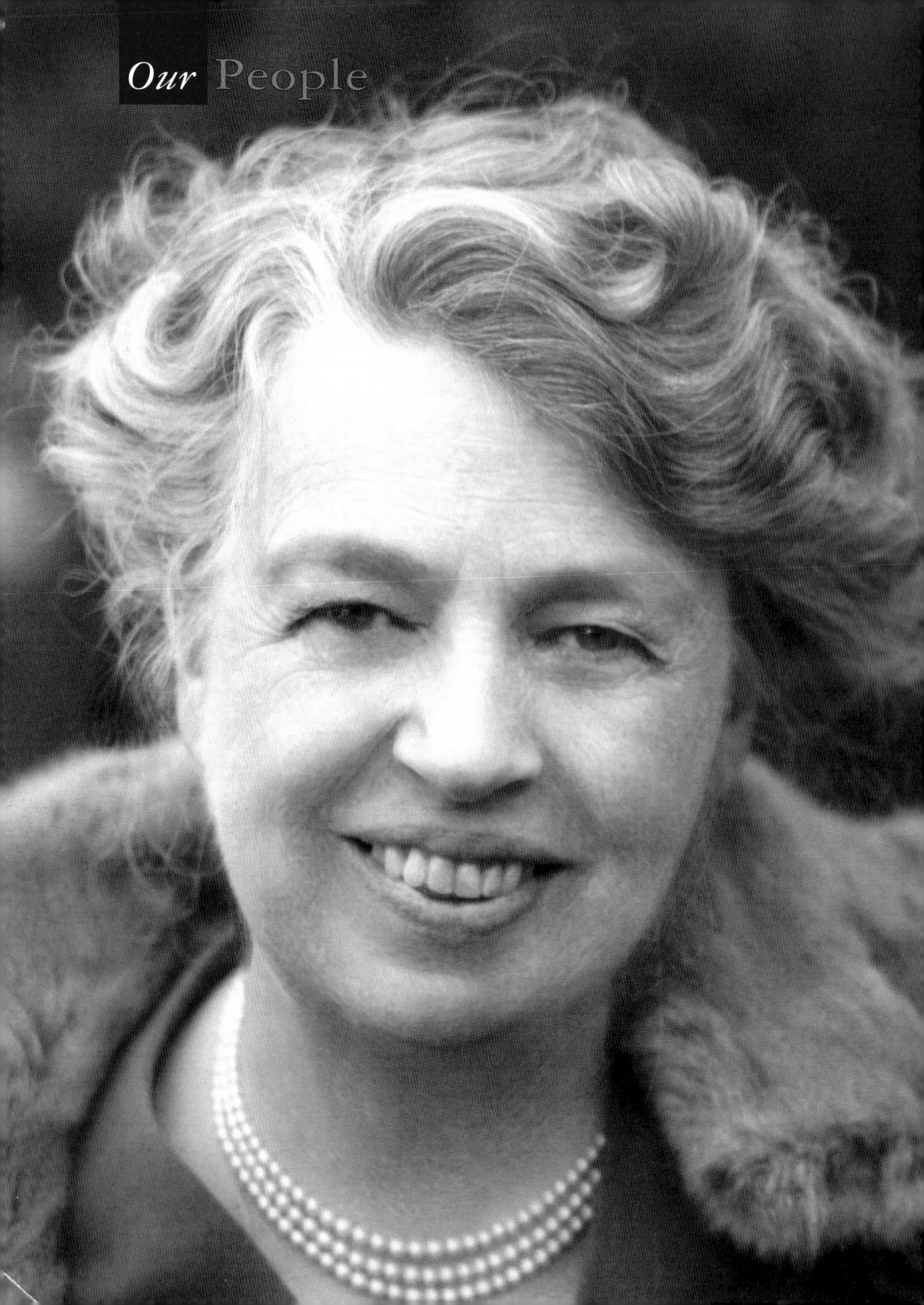

SPIRIT
of America®

ELEANOR *Roosevelt*

FIRST LADY, HUMANITARIAN, AND WORLD CITIZEN

By Pam Rosenberg

Content Adviser: Robin Gerber, Senior Scholar, Academy of Leadership,
University of Maryland, Bethesda, Maryland

The Child's World®
Chanhassen, Minnesota

ELEANOR *Roosevelt*

Published in the United States of America by The Child's World®
PO Box 326 • Chanhassen, MN 55317-0326 • 800-599-READ • www.childsworld.com

Acknowledgments
The Child's World®: Mary Berendes, Publishing Director

Editorial Directions, Inc.: E. Russell Primm, Editorial Director; Pam Rosenberg, Line Editor; Elizabeth K. Martin, Assistant Editor; Olivia Nellums, Editorial Assistant; Susan Hindman, Copy Editor; Susan Ashley, Halley Gatenby, Proofreaders; Jean Cotterell, Kevin Cunningham, Peter Garnham, Fact Checkers; Tim Griffin/IndexServ, Indexer; Dawn Friedman, Photo Researcher; Linda S. Koutris, Photo Selector

Photo
Cover: Stock Montage, Inc.; Air Force Historical Research Agency—Maxwell Air Force Base, AL: 25, AP/Wide World Photos: 19; Corbis: 6, 8, 11; Bettmann/Corbis: 7, 13, 16, 20, 22, 23, 27, 28; Hulton-Deutsch Collection/Corbis: 21; National Park Service, Roosevelt-Vanderbilt National Historic Sites, Hyde Park, NY: 17 bottom; Franklin D. Roosevelt Library, Hyde Park, NY: 9 top and bottom, 10, 12, 14, 15, 17 top, 18, 24, 26; Stock Montage, Inc.: 2.

Library of Congress Cataloging-in-Publication Data
Rosenberg, Pam.
  Eleanor Roosevelt : First Lady, humanitarian, and world citizen / by Pam Rosenberg.
    p. cm. — (Our people)
  "Spirit of America."
  Summary: Provides a brief introduction to Eleanor Roosevelt, her accomplishments, and her impact on American history.
  Includes bibliographical references (p.) and index.
   ISBN 1-59296-001-4 (lib. bdg. : alk. paper)
   1. Roosevelt, Eleanor, 1884–1962—Juvenile literature. 2. Presidents' spouses—United States—Biography—Juvenile literature. [1. Roosevelt, Eleanor, 1884–1962. 2. First ladies. 3. Women—Biography.] I. Title. II. Series.
   E807.1.R48R674 2003
   973.917'092—dc21   2003004159

18　　　　　　　21　　　　　　　26

Contents

Chapter ONE

Child of Privilege

Eleanor Roosevelt was a shy and serious child.

IN 1884, WOMEN DID NOT HAVE THE RIGHT TO VOTE. African-Americans were regularly denied their rights as citizens of the United States. Many people worked long, hard hours in factories for low wages. On October 11 of that year, Eleanor Roosevelt was born. She would spend much of her life working tirelessly on behalf of women, African-Americans, and the working poor.

It would have been easy for Eleanor Roosevelt to ignore people who were less fortunate. She was the first child of Elliott Roosevelt and Anna Hall Roosevelt. Her parents were members of two of the richest families in New York. Still, Eleanor had an unhappy childhood. She and her mother did not have a close relationship. Her mother was a very beautiful woman.

Eleanor was not pretty and was very shy. Her mother often called her Granny because she was always so serious. Eleanor and her father had a very warm, loving relationship. Unfortunately, she did not see her father very often. He was an alcoholic who was frequently away from the family. But Eleanor treasured the time she spent with him. As an adult, she said that he was "the love of her life" as a child.

Eleanor Roosevelt (right) with her father and brothers Elliott and Gracie Hall Roosevelt

When Eleanor was only eight years old, her mother died suddenly. Eleanor and her brothers were sent to live with their grandmother, Mary Ludlow Hall. Then, less than a year later, Eleanor's brother Elliott died. She faced yet another tragedy the following year when her beloved father died. She was heartbroken.

In her autobiography, Eleanor writes of going with her father to help serve Thanksgiving dinner to homeless boys. This and other experiences impressed her as a child. Even then, she realized that there were many people who did not live as well as she did. Perhaps those experiences, combined with facing so many tragic events, helped Eleanor develop her strong desire to help people in need.

Interesting Fact

▸ Eleanor Roosevelt's mother's full name was Anna Rebecca Livingston Ludlow Hall Roosevelt. One of her Livingston ancestors signed the Declaration of Independence. Another of the Livingstons administered the oath of office to George Washington.

▸ Many famous
quotations have been
credited to Eleanor
Roosevelt. They
include: "You must
have skin as thick
as a rhinoceros hide."
"No one can make
you feel inferior with-
out your consent."
"You must do the
thing you think you
cannot do."

In 1899, when Eleanor was 15, she went to England to study at Allenswood School. This was a school run by Marie Souvestre, a Frenchwoman. At a time when it was not considered necessary for girls to be educated, Souvestre encouraged her pupils to learn as much as they could. Eleanor blossomed at the school. She developed a love for learning that lasted her entire life.

In 1902, after three years at Allenswood, Eleanor went home. She was expected to make her debut in society. This meant that she would have to attend many parties and dances. She was not very happy about this, but she did what was expected of her. Eleanor felt there should be more to life than dancing and fun. She joined the Junior League, a group of women who helped poor immigrants. Much of her free time was spent volunteering at the College Settlement House on Rivington Street, where she taught exercise and dance to young immigrant girls. Her work there helped develop her passion for helping people less fortunate than herself.

Many poor immigrants in New York City lived in rundown tenement houses.

She also joined the National Consumer's League. This was a group of women who tried to make working conditions better for the girls and women who worked in garment factories and department stores.

ALLENSWOOD WAS A PRIVATE SCHOOL FOR YOUNG WOMEN. Many wealthy girls from Europe and the United States attended the school. Located outside of London, England, it was founded by Marie Souvestre (left). She thought it was important for young women to be educated.

This belief was not common at the time. Souvestre was a **feminist.** She believed that it was important for women to think for themselves, and she encouraged her students to do so. Eleanor developed a close relationship with Souvestre, even traveling with her during school vacations. The headmistress was not only Eleanor's teacher, but also her **mentor** and friend. Eleanor considered Souvestre to be the one person, besides her father, who most influenced her during the early years of her life.

Chapter TWO

Mrs. Franklin D. Roosevelt

ONE DAY IN THE SUMMER OF 1902, ELEANOR Roosevelt was riding in a train by herself. Franklin Delano Roosevelt, a distant cousin of hers, saw her and asked if she would like to sit with him and his mother. They had seen each other over the years at family gatherings but had not developed a close friendship. That was about to change.

Eleanor and Franklin D. Roosevelt were distant cousins who married in 1905.

Eleanor and Franklin saw each other at many social events over the next several months. Their relationship grew closer, and on November 22, 1903, Franklin proposed to Eleanor. They were married on March 17, 1905, in New York City. Eleanor's uncle, President Theodore Roosevelt, walked her down the aisle. At the time, she didn't imagine that her new husband would one day be president of the United States, too.

Eleanor and Franklin had six children: Anna, James, Franklin Jr. (who died in infancy), Elliott, Franklin Jr., and John. At this stage of her life, much of Eleanor's time was taken up with being a wife and mother. Franklin was an aspiring politician. In 1910, he was elected to the New York state senate, and the family moved to Albany, New York. In 1913, they moved to Washington, D.C., after Franklin was appointed assistant secretary of the navy.

When the United States entered World War I in 1917, Eleanor worked with the Red Cross and the Navy League to help people serving in the U.S. armed forces. Working with the Red Cross was dirty and tiring, and many people criticized Eleanor for it. They thought this kind of work was not suitable for a woman from a wealthy family.

Eleanor and Franklin D. Roosevelt with their five surviving children, Elliott, Franklin Jr., James, John, and Anna

But Eleanor was a compassionate person who was determined to help wounded sailors and their families.

After the war ended, she went to Europe with her husband. She was able to see for herself the horrible effects the war had on people in the countries where it had been fought. This experience strongly affected Eleanor. She became an **advocate** for the League of Nations, a group dedicated to fostering cooperation between nations. She spent much time throughout her life working to bring about world peace.

James Cox and Franklin D. Roosevelt were the Democratic candidates for president and vice president in the 1920 election.

In 1920, the Roosevelts moved back to New York City. That same year, Franklin attended the Democratic National Convention in San Francisco. There he campaigned for Al Smith to be chosen as the party's candidate for president. Smith was not selected. Instead, the members of the party chose James Cox as their presidential candidate. When Cox was picked, he unexpectedly asked Franklin to be his vice presidential candidate. Eleanor went campaigning with him in the fall. She increased her knowledge of politics during this time. She also developed a close friendship with Franklin's longtime political adviser, Louis Howe. He would remain a mentor and friend to Eleanor for many years. The presidential election of November 1920 resulted in disappointment for the Roosevelts, however. Cox and Roosevelt lost in a **landslide.**

Eleanor and Franklin returned to New York. Franklin went back to his law practice. Eleanor continued to care for her family, but she began spending more time pursuing her own political and social causes. Then, in 1921, Franklin became

Louis Howe was Franklin D. Roosevelt's political adviser and a friend and mentor to Eleanor Roosevelt.

Eleanor and her friends Marion Dickerman, Nancy Cook, and Peggy Levenson (Dickerman's sister) on a camping trip in 1926.

sick with polio. He lost the use of his legs, and Eleanor nursed him through his illness. Although he never regained the full use of his legs, Eleanor encouraged him to continue his political career.

At the same time, she continued her own activities. She joined the Women's Trade Union League in 1922. Along with others in this group, she fought for better working conditions for women and children. Eleanor also joined the Women's Division of the New York State Democratic Committee that same year. She believed that it was important for women to be involved in politics and use their newly acquired right to vote to achieve equality. Throughout the 1920s, she would spend much of her time fighting for the causes she believed in.

In 1925, Eleanor, two of her good friends—Marion Dickerman and Nancy Cook—and another woman, Caroline O'Day, started the Val-Kill Industries furniture factory. This factory was located on the grounds of Val-Kill Cottage, a home the Roosevelts built in Hyde Park. Cook ran the factory. Eleanor used money that she earned from radio speeches and writing to help finance the operation of the factory.

Marion Dickerman was the vice principal of a private girls' school in New York City. A few months after the women started Val-Kill, Dickerman had the opportunity to buy the school. Eleanor saw this as a chance to help provide young women with a good education, like the one she had received at Allenswood. She convinced Dickerman that they should purchase the school as partners. The school's name was Todhunter. In addition to all of her political and volunteer activities, Eleanor became a teacher there.

Eleanor Roosevelt enjoyed teaching young women at Todhunter. This photo was taken on a school trip to Mount Vernon.

In 1928, Franklin was elected governor of New York. Eleanor once again moved her family to Albany, the state capital. Her life became even busier. She continued teaching at Todhunter, commuting each week between New York City and Albany. She also continued to champion her own causes and carry out her obligations as the governor's wife.

In 1931, Franklin decided to run for president of the United States. Eleanor spent a great deal of time traveling and giving speeches, especially to women's groups. She did not directly campaign for her husband, but she did speak out about what the Democratic Party stood for and told women that they should think for themselves in political matters. In 1932, Franklin Delano Roosevelt was nominated as the Democratic candidate for president. That November, he won the election. The Roosevelts were on their way to Washington, D.C., again.

VAL-KILL WAS A VERY SPECIAL place for Eleanor Roosevelt. After her mother's death, she went to live with her grandmother. When she married, she moved into homes that were owned by her husband or his mother. Eleanor wanted to have a place she could call her own. Franklin understood this need, and he created the original plans for Val-Kill Cottage.

Franklin chose Elliot Brown to oversee the project. He wrote a letter to Brown that said, "My Missus and some of her female political friends want to build a shack on a stream in the back woods and want, instead of a beautiful marble bath, to have the stream dug out so as to form an old fashioned swimming hole."

In May 1977, President Jimmy Carter made Val-Kill a National Historic Site. It is the only one dedicated to a first lady. Visitors can tour Eleanor's beloved cottage, enjoy the beauty of its surroundings, and learn more about the life and work of Eleanor Roosevelt.

Chapter THREE

First Lady of the United States

Franklin and Eleanor Roosevelt on the day of his inauguration

ELEANOR ROOSEVELT WORKED hard to help her husband become president of the United States, so it was surprising to many people how much she dreaded the thought of becoming first lady. When speaking about her new role, she said, "I knew what traditionally would lie before me, and I cannot say I was very pleased with the prospect."

Eleanor was determined to be a different kind of first lady. Instead of just being the hostess for White House functions, she wanted to continue her many activities. She also did not plan to stop giving her husband and others her opinions on important subjects. She wanted to continue her writing and public speaking. Eleanor knew she would have to give up her teaching position at Todhunter, though, and that troubled her greatly. "I wonder if you have any idea how I hate to do it," she told Lorena Hickok, a news reporter who had been assigned to cover her during the campaign, about giving up that job.

When Franklin D. Roosevelt became president, the country was in the midst of a great **economic depression.** It had started with the stock market crash of October 1929. Many banks and businesses closed, and millions of people were out of work. It was a desperate time for many people in the United States. President Roosevelt created government policies called the New Deal to help bring about an economic recovery and get people back to work. Eleanor had a great deal of input into these policies.

Lorena Hickok was a journalist who became one of Eleanor Roosevelt's closest friends.

When Franklin was governor of New York, it was difficult for him to get around. Eleanor often traveled on his behalf, serving as his "eyes and ears." When she returned, she would answer all of his questions as well as give him her input. As first lady of the United States, Eleanor continued in this role.

But for Eleanor, these trips meant more than just serving as her husband's "eyes and ears." They allowed her to develop her own opinions about what the government should do to help people affected by the depression. Eleanor traveled to coal mines, camps for migrant workers, and the homes of people who lived in **slums.** She saw the crowded dirty places so many people were forced to live in. She heard parents tell stories about the daily struggle to feed their hungry children. As a result, she developed a true understanding of what people in the United States were going through because of the depression.

When Eleanor returned from a trip and sat down with Franklin to discuss her findings, she made sure to express her opinions. In fact, Rexford Tugwell, one of President Roosevelt's top advisers once said, "No one who ever saw Eleanor Roosevelt sit down facing her husband, and holding his eye

Shantytowns such as this one in Seattle, Washington, were often named after President Herbert Hoover and called Hoovervilles.

20

firmly, say to him, 'Franklin, I think you should. . .' or, 'Franklin, surely you will not. . .' will ever forget the experience. . . ." Tugwell and other knew that Franklin greatly respected Eleanor's opinions and was influenced by them.

Eleanor was also not afraid to express her opinions in the many articles and speeches she wrote or in her radio talks. In 1936, she began writing a newspaper column that was published around the country six days a week. The column was called "My Day." Many people came to feel they knew Eleanor, and they believed that she truly understood their needs. She became known as a true **humanitarian.** They wrote letters to her, asking for help. Sometimes Eleanor would send the letters on to people in government positions, with a note asking them if they could do something to help. She shared some of these letters with her husband to help him understand what people in the country were going through.

In December 1941, the United States entered World War II. Eleanor began to work even harder, which was amazing to many people. She worked so

Eleanor Roosevelt often gave talks on the radio.

Interesting Fact

▶ Eleanor Roosevelt had a sense of humor about what was expected of the First Lady. She once said the requirements included the following: Remember to lean back in a parade, so that people can see your husband. Don't get too fat to ride three on a seat.

hard because she felt a strong sense of responsibility to help in any way she could. Eleanor spoke out in favor of making it easier for refugees from Europe to enter the United States. She was particularly concerned about the many people suffering in Germany under the policies of Adolf Hitler.

She had always spoken out in favor of women working outside their homes. During World War II, this became a necessity because so many men were in the armed forces fighting the war. Eleanor supported these working women by helping to create day care centers and kitchens with take-out food in factories. She also spoke out for equal pay for equal work.

Eleanor was a strong advocate for the civil rights of African-Americans, even before the war. In 1934, she joined the National Urban League, and she was often involved with the National Association for the Advancement of Colored People (NAACP). Her position was not very popular. African-Americans in the United States were still seen by many as inferior to white people. They had to fight daily to be

During World War II, many women went to work in factories because so many men were overseas fighting in the war.

treated fairly. During the war, Eleanor worked hard to get her husband to establish a commission to ensure that businesses receiving federal contracts did not **discriminate** against black people. She also spoke out for the equal treatment of blacks in the military.

Eleanor was genuinely grateful to members of the armed forces and their families for the sacrifices they were making. As a mother, she understood only too well the sacrifices being made by mothers all over the nation. When the United States entered the war, all of her sons wanted to serve their country. She was proud, and she knew that they must set an example for everyone in the nation, but that didn't make it any easier to say goodbye to them as they went off to war.

Eleanor wrote back to many soldiers who wrote letters to her during the war. A few of them became her pen pals. Through her **correspondence** with them, she was able to learn more about how to help all soldiers while they were at war. She often wrote about the soldiers and their needs in her "My Day"

Eleanor visits her son, Franklin Delano Roosevelt Jr. during World War II.

Interesting Fact

▶ During World War II, Eleanor Roosevelt carried the following prayer in her purse: Dear Lord, Lest I continue my complacent way, help me to remember, somehow out there, a man dies for me today. As long as there be war, I then must ask and answer am I worth dying for?

column. This helped to inform the public and get government leaders to try to make things better. During the war, Eleanor made many trips to military bases and met thousands of soldiers. She did her best to make sure they knew that she and the millions of people back home appreciated all they were doing to keep the country safe.

On April 12, 1945, Eleanor's life changed forever. That day, her husband, President Franklin D. Roosevelt, suffered a stroke and died. Eleanor mourned the loss of the man who was not only her husband, but also a partner in the many causes she championed.

Eleanor Roosevelt did all she could for U.S. soldiers during World War II.

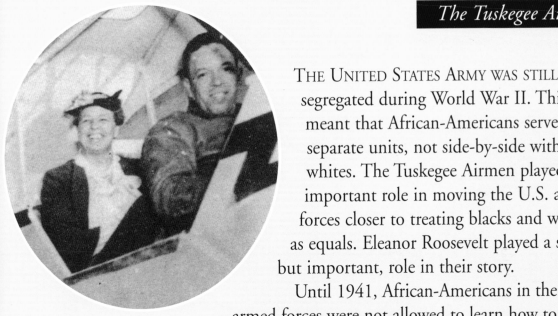

THE UNITED STATES ARMY WAS STILL segregated during World War II. This meant that African-Americans served in separate units, not side-by-side with whites. The Tuskegee Airmen played an important role in moving the U.S. armed forces closer to treating blacks and whites as equals. Eleanor Roosevelt played a small, but important, role in their story.

Until 1941, African-Americans in the armed forces were not allowed to learn how to fly. Many people believed that they did not have the necessary intelligence to operate complicated military planes. In 1941, the army created an African-American unit, which became the 99th Fighter **Squadron.** Top African-American college graduates were chosen to train as pilots. Even though these men were being trained, there was no guarantee that they would see active duty in the war. Many other African-Americans were part of the squadron in support positions on the ground.

Eleanor visited the Tuskegee Army Air Field in 1941. She strongly believed in equal rights for African-Americans. When she arrived, she insisted on riding in an airplane with a black pilot. Charles Anderson, the first African-American to earn a pilot's license and the flight instructor of the Tuskegee pilots, flew the plane. Eleanor made sure that her flight with Anderson was photographed. She had the film developed right away. She took the pictures back to Washington and used them to help convince her husband to send the Tuskegee Airmen off to active duty.

In this way, Eleanor helped make sure these talented men were allowed to contribute to the war effort. And they didn't let her, or their country, down. They flew as protection for American bombers. In more than 1,500 missions, they never lost a bomber to the enemy.

Chapter FOUR

After the White House

After leaving the White House, Eleanor continued to travel around the world. She is shown here on a trip to Japan in 1953.

AFTER FRANKLIN D. ROOSEVELT DIED, POLITICAL party leaders urged Eleanor Roosevelt to run for office. But she did not want to hold any elected position. After leaving the White House, she continued giving lectures and writing her newspaper columns. In addition, she wrote numerous books and articles. She also hosted radio shows and her own television program for a while.

Traveling continued to be important to Eleanor. She traveled all over the world, meeting

with the leaders of many countries. Wherever she went, she spoke out for the rights of all people.

In 1945, President Harry S. Truman signed the United Nations Charter and asked Eleanor to be one of the U.S. delegates to the United Nations. The following year, she became the chairperson of its Human Rights Commission. As the leader of this group, she skillfully guided its members in the creation of the Universal Declaration of Human Rights. This document details the rights that should be guaranteed to all people in all countries.

Eleanor Roosevelt was a member of the U.S. delegation to the United Nations and served as chairperson of its Human Rights Commission.

Interesting Fact

▸ In 1957, the Ku Klux Klan offered a $25,000 reward to anyone who killed Eleanor Roosevelt.

Many dignitaries attended Eleanor Roosevelt's funeral including Jacqueline Kennedy, President John F. Kennedy, Vice-President Lyndon B. Johnson, former President Harry S. Truman and his wife Bess, and former President Dwight D. Eisenhower.

It would be impossible to list all of the things that Eleanor Roosevelt did during her lifetime. Her energy seemed to have no limit. She was a woman of strong opinions. These opinions sometimes brought her great criticism, but they did not stop her from speaking out for and doing what she thought was right. Ill with a rare form of tuberculosis, Eleanor Roosevelt died on November 7, 1962. Millions of people around the world mourned her death. Today, we are still enjoying the benefits of all that she accomplished during her lifetime.

1884   Eleanor Roosevelt is born on October 11 in New York City.

1892   Anna Hall Roosevelt, Eleanor's mother, dies.

1893   Eleanor's brother Elliott dies.

1894   Eleanor's father, Elliott Roosevelt, dies.

1899   Eleanor begins her studies at Allenswood School in England.

1902   Eleanor leaves Allenswood to return to New York and make her debut.

1903   Eleanor and Franklin D. Roosevelt are engaged to be married.

1905   The wedding of Eleanor and Franklin D. Roosevelt takes place on March 17.

1910   Franklin D. Roosevelt is elected to the New York state senate, and the family moves to Albany.

1913   The Roosevelt family moves to Washington, D.C., after Franklin is appointed assistant secretary of the navy.

1917   Eleanor works with the Red Cross and the Navy League to help U.S. servicemen in World War I.

1920   Eleanor campaigns for Franklin, who is the Democratic Party's candidate for vice president.

1921   Franklin D. Roosevelt becomes ill with polio, and Eleanor takes care of him.

1922   Eleanor joins the Women's Trade Union League and the Women's Division of the New York State Democratic Committee.

1925   Val-Kill Cottage is built. The Val-Kill Industries furniture factory is started.

1926   Eleanor begins teaching history and government at the Todhunter School.

1929   Franklin D. Roosevelt becomes governor of New York, and the family moves to Albany again. The U.S. stock market crashes, bringing on the Great Depression.

1932   Franklin D. Roosevelt is elected president of the United States.

1933   The family moves to Washington, D.C., again, and Eleanor becomes first lady.

1934   Eleanor joins the NAACP and the National Urban League.

1936   Franklin D. Roosevelt is reelected.

1940   Franklin D. Roosevelt is elected to a third term as president.

1941   Pearl Harbor is bombed on December 7, and the United States enters World War II. Eleanor travels to meet the Tuskegee Airmen and takes a ride in a plane piloted by Charles Anderson.

1944   Franklin D. Roosevelt is elected president for the fourth time.

1945   Franklin D. Roosevelt dies on April 12. Eleanor is named a member of the U.S. delegation to the United Nations.

1946   Eleanor becomes chairperson of the United Nations Human Rights Commission, which begins work on a declaration of human rights.

1948   The Universal Declaration of Human Rights is presented to the United Nations General Assembly. It is adopted on December 10.

1961   Eleanor becomes the chairperson of the President's Commission on the Status of Women.

1962   Eleanor Roosevelt dies on November 7.

advocate (AD-vuh-kit)
An advocate is one who speaks or writes in support of something. Eleanor became an advocate for the League of Nations.

correspondence (kor-uh-SPON-duhns)
Correspondence is the writing and receiving of letters. Through her correspondence with soldiers at war, Eleanor was able to learn how to help them.

discriminate (diss-KRIM-uh-nate)
To discriminate is to treat certain groups of people less fairly or unequally. Eleanor wanted to ensure that businesses did not discriminate against African-Americans.

economic depression (ek-uh-NOM-ik di-PRESH-uhn)
An economic depression is a period during which there is less business and many people lose their jobs, such as the Great Depression beginning in 1929. Eleanor developed a true understanding of what people were going through because of the economic depression.

feminist (FEM-uh-nist)
A feminist is a person who believes that women should have political, economic, and social rights that are equal to those of men. Marie Souvestre was a feminist.

humanitarian (hyoo-man-uh-TER-ee-un)
A humanitarian is someone who works hard to help all people and relieve human suffering. Eleanor Roosevelt was a true humanitarian.

landslide (LAND-slide)
A landslide involves winning or losing by a great majority of votes. James Cox and Franklin Roosevelt lost to Warren G. Harding and Calvin Coolidge in a landslide.

mentor (MEN-tore)
A mentor is a wise and trusted counselor. Marie Souvestre was not only Eleanor Roosevelt's teacher, but also her mentor.

slums (SLUMZ)
Slums are the parts of a city where many poor people live in crowded, run-down buildings. Eleanor Roosevelt visited the homes of people who lived in slums.

squadron (SKWAHD-ruhn)
A squadron is an organized group of soldiers. The 99th Fighter Squadron became known as the Tuskegee Airmen.

ƆN

about Eleanor Roosevelt:
.html

they're safe,
them out!

Milwaukee, Wis.: World Almanac Library,

A Life of Discovery. New York: Houghton

nd the Arthurdale Experiment. North Haven,

c Site
and to tour Val-Kill Cottage

Library
leanor Roosevelt's life and work

Index

About the Author

PAM ROSENBERG IS A FORMER JUNIOR HIGH SCHOOL TEACHER AND corporate trainer. She currently works as an author and editor of children's books. She has always loved reading and feels very fortunate to be doing work that requires her to read all the time. When she isn't writing or editing books she enjoys spending time with her husband and two children, reading just for fun, and singing with her choir. She lives in Chicago.